Anonymous

Saint Patrick's Cathedral, New York

A full description of the exterior and interior of the new cathedral, the

altars and windows - with biographical sketches of Cardinal McCloskey,

and the Most Rev. Archbishop Hughes, D. D

Anonymous

Saint Patrick's Cathedral, New York
A full description of the exterior and interior of the new cathedral, the altars and windows - with biographical sketches of Cardinal McCloskey, and the Most Rev. Archbishop Hughes, D. D

ISBN/EAN: 9783337272944

Printed in Europe, USA, Canada, Australia, Japan

Cover: Foto ©Lupo / pixelio.de

More available books at **www.hansebooks.com**

"O Lord our God, all this store that we have prepared to build Thee a house for Thy Holy Name is from Thy hand, and all things are Thine."—1 Par. xxix, 16.

———•••——

SAINT PATRICK'S CATHEDRAL,

NEW YORK.

A FULL DESCRIPTION OF THE EXTERIOR AND INTERIOR
OF THE NEW CATHEDRAL, THE ALTARS
AND WINDOWS:

WITH BIOGRAPHICAL SKETCHES OF

His Eminence Cardinal McCloskey,

AND

The Most Rev. Archbishop Hughes, D.D.

———•••——

WEST CHESTER:
THE NEW YORK CATHOLIC PROTECTORY PRINT.
1879.

THE NEW ST. PATRICK'S CATHEDRAL.

CORNER-STONE LAID BY THE MOST REV. ARCHBISHOP HUGHES,
AUGUST 15, 1858.

DEDICATED BY HIS EMINENCE CARDINAL MᶜCLOSKEY,
MAY 25, 1879.

HE 15th of August, 1858, was a memorable day for the Catholic people of New York. On that occasion was laid the corner-stone of this noble Cathedral. One hundred thousand persons were then assembled to witness the ceremony and listen to the magic eloquence of the great prelate whose name will outlast the edifice he labored so faithfully to erect. And no less memorable was the 25th of May, 1879, when His Eminence Cardinal MᶜCLOSKEY, in solemn rite and benediction, surrounded by thirty-six Archbishops and Bishops, more than four hundred Priests, and a vast multitude of the faithful, dedicated this magnificent house of prayer to the honor and service of the living God.

St. Patrick's Cathedral, in its unsurpassed location, in its majestic proportions, is a monument worthy the far-seeing and great mind, the daring, the trust in God and in the generous co-operation of his children, which sum up the character of Archbishop JOHN HUGHES. And true, now, as when the Apostle wrote them, are the words : *"Ego plantavi, Apollo rigavit, Deus autem incrementum dedit"*— to one it is given to begin, to another to carry on and by God's blessing to make perfect; so the first and the second Archbishops stand related and united in nothing more than in this perpetual memorial of their combined zeal for the glory of God's house. To the first Archbishop the honor of origination and inception; to the financial ability, to the unwearied solicitude, the cultivated taste of the second, belong the merit, the glory of completion.

Most Rev. John Hughes, D.D.,

First Archbishop of New York.

Most Rev. John Hughes, D.D.

first Archbishop of New York, was born at Annaloghan, County
Tyrone, Ireland, on the 24th of June, 1797. He was the son of a
farmer in moderate circumstances, and was sent to school near his
native place with a view to his entering the priesthood. In 1816
his father emigrated to America and settled at Chambersburg, Pa.,
and there John joined him the next year, and the rest of the family
the year after. Never, however, losing sight of his vocation for the
priesthood, he proceeded to Emmittsburgh, and in November, 1819,
he was taken into the College of Mount St. Mary, then little more
than a rude academy, under the charge of the Rev. John Dubois,
afterwards Bishop of New York, and the Rev. Simon William
Gabriel Bruté, afterwards Bishop of Vincennes. The friendship of
Fathers Dubois and Bruté proved of the highest advantage to him,
and the saintly Dr. Bruté in particular was his intimate counsellor
through life.

He was ordained deacon in 1825, and on October 15, 1826, was
advanced to the priesthood by Bishop Conwell, at St. Joseph's
Church in Philadelphia. He was first stationed for a few weeks at
St. Augustine's Church in that city, and then placed in charge of
the mission of Bedford, Pennsylvania; but in January, 1827, he was
recalled to Philadelphia and appointed to St. Mary's Church, after-

wards to St. Joseph's. He became highly popular as a preacher
and noted as a controversialist. In 1829 he founded St. John's
Orphan Asylum. In 1831–2 Father Hughes built St. John's
Church, which, under his rectorship, became the favorite Catholic
church of Philadelphia, and was at that time by far the most elegant.
It was soon after his removal to this church that he became involved
in his first celebrated controversy with the Rev. John Breckinridge,
a well-known Presbyterian minister. The dispute was carried on
through the medium of letters, and as there was no Catholic paper
whose columns could be used as Mr. Breckinridge used *The Presbyterian*, Rev. Mr. Hughes established *The Catholic Herald* in
January, 1833. The controversy excited a great deal of interest,
and both sides were afterwards published by Father Hughes. An
oral discussion between the same two champions took place before
a Philadelphia young men's debating society in 1835, and was also
published in book form.

In January, 1838, he was consecrated coadjutor to his old master,
Dr. Dubois, in New York, with the title of Bishop of Basileopolis
in partibus. Powers of administration were conferred upon him in
1839, and on the death of Bishop Dubois, in December, 1842, he
succeeded to the full dignity of Bishop of New York. His rule
from the first was vigorous and active. He put down the preten-
sions of the lay-trustees at the Cathedral, at St. Peter's, and else-
where, founded St. John's College at Fordham (1839), visited
Europe to get money and missionaries for the diocese (1839–40),
and on his return entered into the movement, already started by the
Catholics of New York, to obtain a share of the common-school fund
for the support of their schools. He discussed the whole question
in a memorable debate before the Common Council (October 29
and 30, 1840), in which he opposed, alone, eminent counsel representing the Public School Society, and five prominent clergymen
from various Protestant denominations. Defeated by the Common

Council, he carried the question to the Legislature, and it became an issue in the next election (1841), when the Bishop caused the Catholics to nominate a ticket of their own. The result of the agitation was the overthrow of the Public School Society, and the establishment, substantially, of the system which now prevails.

At the time of the Native-American riots in Philadelphia (1844), when there was danger of similar disturbances in New York, the Bishop prepared to defend the churches by force, and compelled the Mayor to act so vigorously that the rioters were intimidated. Meantime he established schools, continued his battles with unruly trustees, introduced the Jesuits, the Christian Brothers, and other societies, and carried on a number of controversies in the newspapers. During the war with Mexico, President Polk proposed to send him as a special peace envoy to the Mexican republic, but he refused the mission. In 1850 he was appointed Archbishop, and the United States Minister at Rome was instructed from Washington unofficially to urge his creation as cardinal. He had a famous controversy with the Hon. Erastus Brooks respecting the titles to church property (1855), began the new St. Patrick's Cathedral (1858), published a pastoral letter on the temporal power (1860), and at the beginning of the civil war was frequently consulted by President Lincoln and Secretary Seward. In 1861 he was sent by the Government on a special mission to Europe; he visited Paris, Rome, and Ireland; had a long and interesting private interview with the French Emperor and Empress; and after his return, in 1862, an official intimation was conveyed to the Holy See that the President would be greatly pleased to see him made a cardinal. He died January 3, 1864, and was buried at the Cathedral, with extraordinary honors, on the 7th, the courts and public offices being closed on the day of the funeral, and the Legislature and Common Council having passed resolutions of sorrow and condolence.

The Cardinal Archbishop.

His Most Reverend Eminence, John McCloskey, Cardinal of the Holy Roman Church and Archbishop of New York, was born in Brooklyn on the 10th of March, 1810. At that time, and for years afterwards, there was no Catholic church in Brooklyn, and only two in this city. His Eminence, giving the recollections of his boyhood, has beautifully and graphically described the Sunday-morning start for Mass, and the appearance of St. Peter's Church, with its pleasant graveyard amid the green trees which surrounded the unpretending church, the cradle of Catholicity in New York.

He made his classical and theological studies at Mt. St. Mary's College, near Emmittsburg, Md., then under the direction of the saintly Dubois, afterwards Bishop of New York ; thus he not only enjoyed the advantages of being trained in all knowledge and holiness by the eminent scholars whom the French Revolution drove to our shores, but became a connecting link which binds the present state of Catholicity, in its wonderful expansion and growth, with the humble beginnings when the seed was sown of which he has lived to see so abundant a harvest. After a long course of study he was promoted to the sacred priesthood by Bishop Dubois on the 12th

of January, 1834. We may judge the esteem and high appreciation in which the young priest was held from the fact that it had been the Bishop's intention to honor him with the presidency of a new college at Nyack-on-the-Hudson. Unfortunately, just on the eve of his ordination, the building was destroyed by fire. Not daunted by this calamity, the indefatigable prelate resolved to recommence the much-needed institution. The Rev. John McCloskey, in order to pursue still further his studies, and the better to prepare himself for the office before him, solicited and obtained permission to go to Rome. Here, in the very atmosphere of faith and sacred science, he imbibed that store of learning—deep, accurate, finished, of which his career has afforded such constant manifestations and such happy results.

Meanwhile difficulties had arisen which led to the postponement, and finally to the abandonment, of the proposed college; and, on his return, after an absence of more than two years, the young priest received the rectorship of St. Joseph's Church, in this city. In 1841 he was named rector of the Diocesan Seminary, and president of the college lately established at Fordham, whilst he retained the parochial charge of St. Joseph's. But these offices were soon to be exchanged for others more elevated and onerous.

The responsibility and duties of a diocese which embraced the entire State of New York were too pressing for any one man, however energetic; and, at the request of Bishop Hughes, Rome named the Rev. John McCloskey his coadjutor with right of succession, and on the tenth of March, 1844, his thirty-fourth birthday, he was consecrated Bishop of Axiere, *in partibus infidelium,* and Coadjutor of New York.

The surprisingly rapid growth of Catholicity soon necessitated a division of the diocese, and accordingly, in 1847, the new sees of Buffalo and Albany were created; and in May, 1847, Bishop McCloskey was translated to the latter. Here, for seventeen years, he labored; and his toil had its reward, as the flourishing state of the diocese at the close of his administration was most consoling and convincing proof.

When God called the illustrious and indefatigable Archbishop Hughes to his well-earned crown, the Holy See but carried out his request, and confirmed the unanimous vote of the bishops of the province, in appointing Bishop McCloskey to the vacant see. His coming among us was welcomed with deep joy and singular gratification. Here he had been known and admired from childhood; here he had been baptized, confirmed, ordained priest, and consecrated bishop; here he had exercised both sacerdotal and episcopal ministry; ours he was by many claims and titles, and most fitting was it that they should be renewed and made stable and perfect.

He was called to share in the government of the Universal Church by Pius IX., of immortal memory, who created him Cardinal in the Consistory of March 15, 1875.

Of the success and blessings which have attended his kind and wise government among us this is not the place to speak. The New Cathedral so auspiciously completed is of itself a proof that the blessing of God has rested on the labor of his hands.

Under him the work was recommenced so gradually, yet so steadily, that, amid the many calls on Catholic charity and the pressing needs of the particular parishes, the collections made for the Cathedral were responded to, not simply with a sense of duty, but with pleasure and pride, as the building grew apace.

The deep interest manifested by His Eminence in this work deserves particular mention. From the first he made himself familiar with the plans in their minutest detail; it has been his custom and relaxation to visit the Cathedral several times a week, and in person to inspect the work. In his trip to Europe in 1874, and again in 1877, it was one of the main objects to procure and make arrangements for such parts as were under construction : such as altars, the sanctuary decorations, the windows, etc.

His latest and most successful effort to secure the speedy completion of the building was the holding of a mammoth fair, which was inaugurated by Mayor Ely in the presence of many ecclesiastical and civil dignitaries. His Eminence, in addressing the assemblage present on the opening night, which exceeded twenty-five thousand persons, characterized the fair as a work not of mere pleasure, but of true zeal and charity, and urged the necessity of whole-souled co-operation. And not in vain, for the citizens of New York, proverbially liberal, generously responded, especially our own people, and the fair netted one hundred and seventy-five thousand dollars.

The Facts About the Cathedral Property.

It is remarkable with what tenacity an erroneous impression will keep possession of the public mind. It is doubtless the firm belief of nine-tenths of the Protestant community, that the valuable blocks of land, now the property of St. Patrick's Cathedral, were, in some mysterious and indescribable way, obtained as a gift or grant, without consideration, or at least without full consideration, from the city government.

The history of this property is briefly as follows: The block of ground—now made two blocks by the opening of Madison avenue—bounded by Fifth avenue, Fiftieth streeet, Fourth avenue and Fifty-first street, was conveyed by the Mayor, Aldermen and Commonalty of the City of New York to Robert Sylburn, on the 1st of May, 1799, for £405 ($1,012 50), and a reservation of an annual rent of four bushels of wheat. This rent was afterwards (in 1852) commuted by the payment of the further sum of $83 32.

Robert Sylburn conveyed the property to Francis Thompson by deed on the 20th of February, 1810.

Francis Thompson and Thomas Cadle conveyed the same by deed, dated March 1, 1810, to Andrew Morris and Cornelius Heeney.

Andrew Morris and Cornelius Heeney conveyed the same to

Dennis Doyle by deed, dated May 21, 1821; but it had in the meantime been mortgaged by Morris and Heeney to the Eagle Fire Insurance Company of New York, which mortgage was foreclosed by a decree of the Vice-Chancellor, dated September 13, 1828. Under this decree the property was sold by C. F. Grim, Master in Chancery, to Francis Cooper, by deed dated November 12, 1829, for $5,500.

Francis Cooper conveyed the property to the trustees of St. Patrick's Cathedral in the city of New York, and the trustees of St. Peter's Church in the city of New York, by deed, on the 30th January, 1829, for the same that he gave for it, adding interest.

The trustees of St. Peter's Church on the 13th September, 1844, assigned the property, for the benefit of their creditors, to John Powers and C. C. Pise. C. C. Pise, by order of the Supreme Court, transferred the property in October, 1851, to R. J. Bailey and J. B. Nicholson, Pise having resigned and Powers having died.

In 1852 there was a partition suit in the Supreme Court to determine the interest of St. Patrick's Cathedral in the property, and it was decided that one-half belonged to St. Patrick's, and the other half, belonging to St. Peter's, was sold at public auction for the benefit of the creditors of that Church, and was bought by the trustees of St. Patrick's Cathedral for $59,500.

In the same year an exchange of gores was made between the city and St. Patrick's Cathedral, the city conveying a gore on the north side of Fiftieth street, ten inches wide on Fifth avenue, and running to five feet six inches on Fourth avenue; and the Cathedral conveying to the city a similar gore on the north side of Fifty-first street, commencing at a point on Fifth avenue and running to four feet eight inches on Fourth avenue.

Thus it will be seen that the property which now belongs to the Cathedral was first purchased in 1829 by Francis Cooper for St. Peter's Church and St. Patrick's Cathedral, at a chancery sale, for $5,500, and that in 1852 St. Patrick's Cathedral bought the one-half interest of St. Peter's Church in the property at public auction for $59,500.   This is the whole truth in regard to a matter in reference to which there is so much both of innocent and wilful misrepresentation.

The Cathedral.

St. Patrick's Cathedral is an example of the Decorated and Geometric style of Gothic architecture which prevailed in Europe from 1275 to 1400, and of which the cathedrals of Rheims, Amiens, and Cologne, on the Continent of Europe, and the naves of York minster, Exeter, and Westminster, are among the most advanced examples. Though the Cathedral of New York is in this style, its design is as original and distinct as that of any of the above cathedrals; for they, though in the same style of architecture, nevertheless have each the individual stamp of the genius and thought of their originators.

The original plans were drawn by the architect, Mr. James Renwick, in 1853, and adopted by Archbishop Hughes, who contemplated a larger building than the one now erected. In 1857 the Archbishop directed the architect to reduce its dimensions: to take off the side aisle round the apse, and the apsidial chapel, and sacristies, as the ground covered by them would be required for the residences of the Archbishop and canons. These alterations being decided upon, the building commenced, and has been carried on ever since, under the supervision of Mr. Renwick and his associate, Mr. Rodrigue, until the illness which terminated fatally rendered it impossible for the latter to give personal attention to business of any kind.

Europe can boast larger cathedrals; but, for purity of style, originality of design, harmony of proportions, beauty of material, and finish of workmanship, New York Cathedral stands unsurpassed. It is an ornament to the city, an edifice of which every citizen of our great metropolis may well feel proud. A proof that American architects and American artisans can hold their own with the architects and artisans of the Old World; and a proof, also, that the Catholics of New York, in the nineteenth century, are animated by the same spirit that, in the ages of faith, reared the sacred structures that have excited the admiration and wonder of cultivated and uncultivated minds for centuries.

DIMENSIONS OF THE BUILDING.

EXTERIOR.

Extreme length,	332 feet.
Extreme breadth,	174 "
General "	132 "
Towers at base,	32 "
Height of towers,	330 "
Central door,	30 ft. wide, 51 " high.
Width of front between towers,	105 "

INTERIOR.

Length,	306 feet.
Breadth of nave and choir { excluding chapels,	96 "
{ including "	120 "
Length of transept,	140 "
Central aisle,	48 ft. wide, 112 " high.
Side aisles,	24 ft. " 54 " "
Chapels,	18 ft. wide, 14 ft. high, 12 " deep.

THE EXTERIOR OF THE CATHEDRAL.

The block upon which the Cathedral stands is rocky; in many places the rock coming nearly up to the surface, and in others, especially at the south transept, the rock being more than twenty feet below the surface level. Before commencing the foundation-walls, the rock was in all cases cut into steps affording a level and true bed for the cutting course.

The foundations are of very large blocks of blue gneiss, which were laid by derricks in cement mortar up to the level of the surface.

Above the ground-line, the first base course is of Dix Island granite from Maine, as is also the first course under all the columns and marble works of the interior. Above this base course the whole exterior of the building is of white marble from the quarries at Pleasantville, Westchester County, N. Y., and Lee, in Massachusetts, both of which are of excellent quality and color. The whole building is backed in with brick and stone masonry, with hollows in the walls for prevention of dampness and for ventilation, and is constructed in the most careful manner, so that probably no building in this country is more stable, no crack having ever occurred in any part of the whole structure.

The principal front, on Fifth Avenue, may be described as consisting of a central gable, with a tower and spire on each side of it. The gable will be 156 feet in height, and the towers and spires each 330 feet in height.

The grand portal in the lower division of the central gable has its jambs richly decorated with columns with foliage capitals, and has clustered mouldings, with rich ornaments in the arch, which is also decorated and fringed with a double row of foliated tracery, the thickness of the wall being 12 feet 6 inches, and the whole surface or depth of the door being encrusted with marble. It is intended at some future period to place the statues of the Twelve Apostles in the coves of the jambs of this portal in rich tabernacles of white marble. A transom of beautiful foliage, with emblematic designs, crosses the opening of the door at the spring line of the arch, over which a window, with beautiful tracery, fills in the tym·panum or arch.

The gablet over the main portal is richly panelled with tracery, having a shield, bearing the arms of the Diocese, in the central panel. The label over the gable is crocketed with crockets of a very beautiful and original design of the grape-vine and morning-glory, intertwined and alternating in the crockets, and the whole is terminated by a very rich and beautiful finial.

The door is flanked on either side by buttresses terminating in panelled pinnacles, and between these buttresses and the tower buttresses are niches for statues.

The horizontal balustrade over the first story is of rich pierced tracery. Over this and across the whole gable, except where interspersed by the gable over the central portal, is a row of niches, 7 feet 6 inches high, for statues. These niches are decorated by columns with foliage capitals and gablets, with tracery and finials, and are here-after to be filled with statues of saints and martyrs. Above these niches a richly moulded Gothic jamb, with an equilateral arch, encloses a magnificent rose window, 26 feet in diameter, a marvel of Gothic tracery of beautiful and original design, equalling those of the greatest of the cathedrals of Europe.

Above this window the main gable is carried up to the roof lines, and is veiled by a pierced screen of rich tracery, terminated by a label-cornice which is crocketed. The crockets are designed from the leaves and flowers of the passion flower, and rise up the gable, and entwine and support a beautiful foliated cross with the emblem of the Sacred Heart at the intersection of its arms. On either side of the jambs of the central window are buttresses, terminated by pinnacles, and between these and the buttresses of the tower are rich Gothic panels, terminated by crocketed gablets.

The towers on either side of the central gable are 32 feet square at the base, exclusive of the great buttresses, having walls of immense thickness and solidity. The towers maintain the square form for the height of 136 feet, where they change into octagonal lanterns which are 54 feet high, over which are the spires, 140 feet in height, making the total height of each tower and spire, 330 feet. The towers are divided into three stories, the first containing portals corresponding in architecture to the central portal, with crocketed gablets, having tracery and shields containing the arms of the United States and the State of New York, over which are balustrades of pierced tracery. In the second story are windows with richly-moulded jambs and beautiful tracery, corresponding to the great central rose, and terminated by gablets of pierced tracery. The third story will have four small windows on each side, and will be terminated by a label-mould cornice and pierced battlement.

The towers are flanked by massive buttresses decorated with very light and beautiful tabernacles at each offset, and will be terminated by clustered pinnacles, which will join the buttresses of the octagonal lanterns over the towers.

The octagonal lanterns have windows with fine tracery on each side, over which are gablets with traceries, and the whole terminated by cornices and pierced battlements. The eight corner buttresses will be terminated by pinnacles.

The spires will be octagonal in two stories. The first story will have rich moulding in the angles, and the faces will be panelled with traceries. The single columns will be terminated by capitals supporting gablets with finials. The second story will be moulded and panelled like the first story, and will terminate in a magnificent foliage finial carrying the terminal crosses, which will be of copper. Circular stone stairways are carried up in the buttresses of the towers, which will communicate with the organ galleries and upper stories of the towers. It is proposed to place a chime of bells in the third story of the tower at a height of 110 feet above the grade of the Avenue.

The side aisles of the nave behind the towers, and facing the two streets, are divided by buttresses with niches and pinnacles into five bays. Each bay is pierced by a window 13 feet 6 inches wide and 27 feet in height, divided into three bays by mullions, and having the tympanum or arch filled with traceries of rich and varied design. The transept fronts are divided into a central aisle 48 feet wide and 170 feet high, to the top of the crosses of the gables, and two side aisles. The central aisles are marked on the first story by portals corresponding to those of the front, and flanked by buttresses with pinnacles, with panelled gables over the doors, and pierced battlements. Over each door the great transept windows fill the whole space up to the springing of the gables. These two great windows are 28 feet in width by 58 feet in height, and are divided by clustered mullions into six bays, and the tympana or arches are filled with traceries of the richest design. The gablet over the window is richly panelled. A row of niches crosses each transept at the eave-line, and above this the gable is richly panelled with pinnacles and pierced battlements, and is terminated by an octagonal pinnacle and foliated cross. The side aisles of the transept are marked by windows similar to those of the side aisles, and flanked by octagonal buttresses, in which are spiral stairs leading to the triforium and roofs.

The side aisle of the sanctuary has three bays similar to those of the nave. The side aisle of the rear has five bays. The clerestory, which rises 38 feet above the roof of the side aisles, and is 104 feet high to the eaves above the ground-line, is divided into six bays in the nave, two bays in either transept, and three bays in the sanctuary. The apside has five bays, its ground-plan being half a decagon. The bays are divided by buttresses, terminated by grand pinnacles, which rise 30 feet above the eaves. Each bay is pierced by a window 14 ft. 6 in. broad and 26 ft. high, divided by mullions into four bays, and having rich tracery of varied designs in the tympana. The windows are surmounted by panelled gablets with traceries, and the walls between the gablets and pinnacles are finished by pierced battlements. The roofs of the side aisles and clerestories are slated, and the clerestory roof is terminated by a rich metal cresting 5 ft. 6 in. high, having the leaves and flowers gilded, with a central finial at the intersection of the nave and transepts 15 feet in height, decorated with foliage and flowers, and terminated by a cross at the east end of the roof over the apside. The cross is 13 feet in height, and gilt with flowers and foliage ornaments.

The windows are glazed by two thicknesses of sash and glass, set two inches apart, in order to produce an even temperature and prevent drafts of air in the interior of the building. The exterior sashes are glazed with figured glass in lead sash; and the interior sashes with stained glass of the richest description and most beautiful and appropriate designs.

THE INTERIOR OF THE CATHEDRAL.

The interior of the Cathedral, like its exterior, is cruciform, divided in its ground-plan into a nave, two transepts, and a choir or sanctuary. The nave of the Cathedral, or the entire portion between the transepts and Fifth avenue, is 164 feet long, 96 feet wide between the side-aisle walls, 124 feet broad from out to out, including the side-aisle chapels. It is divided longitudinally into seven bays or divisions, defined by the columns, each bay being 23 feet in length, except the first one, between the front towers, which is 26 feet long. In its cross-section the nave consists of a

centre aisle, 48 feet wide and 110 feet in height from the floor to the
apex of the groined ceiling.   The two side aisles are each 24 feet in
width and 54 feet high.   The chapels, which are under the window-
sills of the side aisles, are 14 feet in width and 18 feet high.   The
transepts, or arms of the cross, are 144 feet long, and are divided into
a centre and two side aisles of the same dimensions as those of the
nave.   The choir, or sanctuary, is 95 long, and has a centre aisle
of the same dimensions as that of the nave and four side aisles,
making a total width of 124 feet from wall to wall.   The choir has
three bays and is terminated at the east end by a five-sided apside
in the central aisle.

The columns dividing the central aisle from the side aisles are of
white marble, 35 feet in height and clustered, having four main
columns at the angles, twelve inches in diameter, and eight columns
six inches in diameter attached to the central shaft, giving a combined diameter of five feet, and are ornamented with beautiful foliated capitals.   The arches between the columns, and supporting
the triforium and clerestory, are richly moulded, and rise to the
height of 54 feet.   The space between these arches and the clerestory
windows is 16 feet in height.   This is called the triforium, and is
covered by the roof of the side aisles.   The walls of the nave are
pierced in the triforium by four arches, corresponding to the bays
or divisions of the clerestory windows.   A floor is laid over the
side aisle arches, affording a passage in the triforium all around the
building, at an elevation of 56 feet above the floor of the Cathedral.
The clerestory windows come above, and are a continuation of the
tracery of the triforium.   They are each 14 feet 6 inches in width,
and 26 feet high.

The ceiling of the centre aisle is groined with richly moulded
ribs and jack-ribs, with foliage bosses at their intersections.   The
spring-line of the ceiling is 77 feet from the floor of the Cathedral.
The side-aisle chapel ceilings are also richly groined with ribs and

jack-ribs. Holes, one inch and a half in diameter, are pierced through all the groined ceilings of the building, through which ropes can be let down to suspend scaffolding or men for the purpose of repairing or cleaning the building.

The floors of the nave and transepts will have 408 pews, varying in length from 8 to 11 feet, and having a seating capacity of about 2,500. They will be divided by aisles, varying in width from 7 to 8 feet. The sanctuary floor will be raised six steps above the floor of the Cathedral, and the high altar will be three steps higher, or nine steps above the main floor. The steps will be of grey marble and the platform in front of altar, of richly colored marbles.

The massive doors—heavily panelled, and displaying consummate workmanship—the handsome pews, the front of the organ gallery, and all the woodwork is of white ash.

The building is lighted by gas, disposed as follows: The body of the Cathedral is illuminated by jets placed over the caps of the great central columns, forty-two jets to each column. In addition to these, there are twenty-five jets over the four columns in the side aisles at the intersection of the nave and transepts, and sixty jets placed on the sills of the two great transept windows. There are also forty jets placed behind the two columns in front of the high altar. The chapels, triforium, and circular stairs are also lighted by gas. The total number of jets will be about 1,800.

The whole building is heated by steam from two boilers, placed in a vault in the rear of the Cathedral, on Fifty-first street, from which lines of wrought-iron pipe are carried through a vault into the building and distributed by means of radiators placed against the walls, in the body of the house, and by coils placed under the sanctuary floor. For the heating of the clerestory, coils of pipe are carried all around the walls of the triforium over the side aisle arches.

THE ALTARS.

𝕿𝖍𝖊 𝕳𝖎𝖌𝖍 𝕬𝖑𝖙𝖆𝖗, erected at the east end of the edifice, in the centre aisle of the choir, stands thirty feet distant from the east wall of the Cathedral. The reredos, or altar-screen, thirty-three feet in width and fifty feet in height to the top of the centre pinnacle, was carved and finished in Poitiers stone, at St. Brieuc, in France. It is presented by the clergy of the Archdiocese. The centre tower of the reredos has a niche containing a statue of our Lord, and the two flanking towers bear statues of St. Peter and St. Paul. Over these statues the towers rise and are crowned with pierced spires of open tracery-work. The spaces between the central and the two corner towers are divided into six niches, three on either side of the centre, containing angelic figures bearing emblems of the Passion.

The altar proper was constructed in Italy, together with the tabernacle and stylobate, or lower division of the reredos. These are all of the purest Italian marble, inlaid with alabasters and precious marbles. The front of the bottom part of the altar is divided into niches and panels; the niches containing statues of the four Evangelists, the panels representing in bas-reliefs the Last Supper, the Carrying of the Cross, the Agony in the Garden,—all in the purest Carrara marble. The tabernacle on the altar is of marble, decorated with Roman mosaics, flanked by columns of rare and costly marbles, and has a door of gilt bronze set with emeralds and garnets. It is the gift of His Eminence Cardinal McCloskey.

A crypt or vault for the entombing of the Archbishops of New York is constructed under the floor of the sanctuary, at a distance of ten feet from the front of the high altar. The crypt is lined with stone of different colors and white marble. It is of sufficient capacity to contain forty-two coffins.

𝕿𝖍𝖊 𝕬𝖑𝖙𝖆𝖗 𝖔𝖋 𝖙𝖍𝖊 𝕭𝖑𝖊𝖘𝖘𝖊𝖉 𝖁𝖎𝖗𝖌𝖎𝖓 is placed at the eastern end of the north side aisle of the sanctuary. The tabernacle and reredos, carved in French oak, are filled with beautiful figures crowned by pierced spires. The reredos is flanked by two ornamental niches, with statues of St. Joachim and St. Anne. The altar, of Poitiers stone, has its front delicately carved and sculptured into panels containing, in bas-reliefs, the Birth of our Lord, the Annunciation, the Descent from the Cross. The tabernacle, carved in severe style, and the two angels standing on either side bearing censers, are of white marble.

𝕿𝖍𝖊 𝕬𝖑𝖙𝖆𝖗 𝖔𝖋 𝖙𝖍𝖊 𝕾𝖆𝖈𝖗𝖊𝖉 𝕳𝖊𝖆𝖗𝖙 in the south transept is of bronze very elaborately ornamented. Over the tabernacle our Lord stands on a pedestal or base, supported by two kneeling angels; on either side of the tabernacle are represented in bas-reliefs the Last Supper and the Apparition of our Lord to Mother Margaret Alacoque. In front are four statues representing the sacrifices of the old dispensation, and in the middle our Lord holds a chalice. Columns of Egyptian granite with capitals and pedestals of white marble stand on either side. They are surmounted by bronze statues of St. Peter and St. Paul, a gift from His Holiness Pius IX. to His Eminence the Cardinal. This altar is the gift of His Eminence Cardinal McCloskey.

𝕿𝖍𝖊 𝕬𝖑𝖙𝖆𝖗 𝖔𝖋 𝖙𝖍𝖊 𝕳𝖔𝖑𝖞 𝕱𝖆𝖒𝖎𝖑𝖞 is in the north transept. The reredos which is of Caen stone is very beautifully and elaborately ornamented. It is divided into three panels, the centre panel having an exquisite oil painting of the Holy Family by Castaggini, New York. Carved on the oaken door of the Tabernacle are clustering grapes and wheat, representing the bread and wine used in the Holy Sacrifice of the Mass. This Altar is the gift of Joseph Donohue, San Francisco.

𝕾𝖙. 𝕵𝖔𝖘𝖊𝖕𝖍'𝖘 𝕬𝖑𝖙𝖆𝖗 stands in front of the west wall of the sacristy, and is of bronze and mosaic. Three scenes are represented on its front. In the middle the Archangel Gabriel announces the mystery of the Incarnation to the Blessed Virgin ; on the Gospel side St. Joseph teaches the infant Jesus his trade, and on the Epistle side St. Anne instructs the child Mary.   This altar, together with the window of St. Agnes above, is the gift of Mrs. Agnes Maitland.

In addition to the above altars there will be eight altars in the chapels under the side windows of the nave.

The Archbishop's throne, erected against the first column inside of the sanctuary, on the Gospel side, is of carved French oak. Over the seat is a magnificent Gothic canopy, supported by columns of the same style, and crowned by an octagonal lantern ornamented with statues, crockets, finials, and angelic figures of the most beautiful design and workmanship.

The handsome sanctuary-rail, of polished brass, branching out from the first columns of the sanctuary, forms an elliptical curve. The design consists of highly ornamented pillars, from which spring wide arches; on the summits of the pillars, at the junction of the arches, are inserted intricate ornaments of delicate execution, prominently exhibiting the oak-leaf and the acorn.   It is similar on both sides, and surmounted by a massive oak strip.

The temporary sacristy is placed in the two most easterly bays of the south side aisle of the sanctuary.   It is forty-eight feet in length and twenty-eight in width, and is divided from the rest of the Cathedral by a low wall.

----✠----

THE WINDOWS.

As a collection, there is nothing, perhaps, in painted glass in modern times to compare with the windows of St. Patrick's Cathedral. Here and there in some convent chapel or in a church there is a beautiful specimen of glass; but for size, number, richness of coloring, variety, and artistic beauty, those which flood this vast Cathedral with their dim religious light stand altogether unrivalled.

It is a matter of sincere congratulation that all its figured windows have been executed in that country where the most precious treasures of the art survive—in France—and that almost all of them were made under the very shadow of the Cathedral of Chartres, where, it is universally admitted, the most beautiful specimens of the thirteenth century painted glass are preserved.

There are in all seventy windows in the new Cathedral. Of these thirty-seven are figured, *i e.*, represent scenes from scripture and from the lives of the saints; twenty are filled with what is termed cathedral stained glass, having only geometrical figures; and the remainder being needed for the purpose of lighting portions of the building where use, not ornament, is the object in view, are filled with white glass.

Of the figured, the two great windows of the transept, are storied windows; so-called because they give the history or story of a life, told in a series of scenes—a sort of epic in stained glass. Of these the six-bayed window over the south transept door is first entitled to mention, being the titular window of the Cathedral.

THE WINDOW OF ST. PATRICK.

Here we have the whole life of St. Patrick succinctly told in eighteen scenes, beginning with his baptism and ending with his death. We shall content ourselves with giving the inscriptions under each scene, and pointing out the order in which they are to be read.

Beginning at the base of the left hand bay, and reading the scenes upward in lines of three each, we find : 1. The baptism of St. Patrick; 2. He is taken prisoner at the age of thirteen ; 3. An angel reveals to him his vocation; 4. He preaches the gospel on board a ship; 5. He is sold to King Milcho; 6. He is set at liberty at Maestric; 7. He is made a cleric by his uncle, St. Martin Bishop of Tours; 8. He pursues his studies in the island of Lerins; 9. He is ordained a priest by Bishop Sancaur; 10. He sets out for Rome; 11. He receives the blessing of Pope Celestine; 12. He is consecrated Bishop by St. Amataur; 13. He visits St. Germain d'Auxerre; 14. He converts Dichu and his family (on his arrival in Ireland); 15. He gives Holy Communion to the princesses Ethna and Fethlema; 16. He raises Malfric from the dead; 17. The Saint's death; 18. The angels singing his funeral dirge.

In the centre of the tracery is the beautifully executed scene of St. Patrick's coronation in heaven. Around this scene, in the spandrels, hovers a circle of angels, copied after Fra Angelico, each holding a scroll on which one of the following lines is inscribed, and all of which taken together make a hymn of sweet and simple latinity, descriptive of the glories of heaven. We give the hymn entire, and with it a beautiful and faithful translation not less poetical than the original :—

Quae felix illa civitas!
In qua jugis solemnitas,
Et quam jucunda curia!
Quae curae prorsus nescia.

Illic patres dispositi,
Nec fraus, nec terror hostium.
Sed una vox laetantium,
Et unus ardor cordium.

Nec languor hic, nec senium.
Pro qualitate meriti,
Fruuntur nec fastidiunt,
Qui frui magis sitiunt.
Mirantur nec deficiunt
In illum quem prospiciunt.

Semota jam caligine,
  Lumen vident in lumine,
  Nunc revelata facie
  Regem cernunt in gloria.

How fair that City of the Blest!
  One Festival forever there,
The Church, triumphant and at rest,
  Rules her wide realm without a care,

Enthronéd there the Fathers reign,
  Their combat o'er with foes of truth,
All voices blend in joyous strain,
  From one full heart of ceaseless youth.

Nor strength can fail, nor time prevail,
  Each soul in meed of merit's due,
Receives its fill; and, sateless still,
  With thirst and relish ever new,
Drinks in a joy that cannot cloy
  The vision freshening to the view.

Eternal Beauty meets their sight;
  Not dimly now by faith and grace,
They see the Primal Light in light,
  Their King in glory face to face.

This window is from the *ateliers* of Mr. Ely, of Nantes, France. The execution of the scenes is as true as an oil painting, even to the perspective, so difficult to realize in stained glass. It is seen to best advantage under the early evening light, just before the sun goes down.

This window is the gift of " The Old St. Patrick's Cathedral to the New," and is a graceful tribute to her more accomplished offspring from the parent church, who is so soon to lay aside the honors of a cathedral, which she has worn with so much glory, through storm and sunshine, during the lapse of more than half a century.

THE WINDOW OF THE BLESSED VIRGIN.

The window is located over the north transept door. Like the corresponding one in the south transept, it, too, is a storied window, giving the whole life, death, assumption, and coronation of the Blessed Virgin in nineteen scenes. These scenes are read from left to right in lines of six each. Beginning at the bottom of the left hand bay, we find: 1. The nativity of the Blessed Virgin Mary; 2. Her presentation in the temple; 3. She is taught by St. Anne; 4. She is espoused to St. Joseph; 5. The Annunciation; 6. The angel appears to St. Joseph in his sleep; 7. The Blessed Virgin visits St. Elizabeth; 8. The Nativity of our Lord; 9. The Shepherds adore the Infant Jesus in the arms of Mary; 10. Adoration of Jesus by the Magi; 11. The presentation of the Infant Jesus in the temple; 12. The flight into Egypt; 13. Joseph carries the Infant Jesus during the journey; 14. The Holy Family in Nazareth; 15. The Mother of Sorrows; 16. Descent of the Holy Ghost upon Mary and the Apostles; 17. Death of the Blessed Virgin; 18. The Assumption.

High above in the centre of the tracery is the scene of our Lady's coronation. She is kneeling in an attitude of ·profound humility, while her divine Son, all radiant with joy, places the crown upon her head. The Holy Ghost, under the form of a dove, hovers above the Mother and Son, while higher still is seen the figure of the Eternal Father looking down " well-pleased " on the scene. These scenes are as delicately finished as miniatures, and will bear as close inspection. The mosaic portions of the work exceed, in richness and softness of tone, anything of the kind in the Cathedral. In the tracery around the coronation scene, the trefoils, etc., are filled with the symbols of the various titles of the Blessed Virgin as found in her litany. Owing to its northern location this window is seen to advantage at any hour of the day. It is said by many, and not without reason, to be the gem of the collection. This and all the windows of the sanctuary, on which we shall touch next, are from the *ateliers* of M. Lorin of Chartres. It is the gift of the Right Rev. Bishop and Clergy of the diocese of Albany, whose cathedral was built and dedicated to our Blessed Lady by his Eminence he Cardinal Archbishop of New York, the first bishop of Albany.

THE WINDOWS OF THE SANCTUARY.

Turning towards the sanctuary, which next claims our attention, we find in the clerestory eleven windows. Of these the six lateral windows represent subjects relating to sacrifice—three on each side. The remaining five windows of the apse, or curve of the sanctuary, contain subjects taken from the History of our Blessed Lord. Beginning with the windows of the sacrifice, and following the chronological order, we find that the first on the north side contains

THE SACRIFICE OF ABEL.

In the foreground are seen the first two sons of Adam tending each an altar. The whole is a graphic rendering of the scriptural history—"And it came to pass, after many days, that Cain offered of the fruits of the earth gifts to the Lord. Abel also offered of the firstlings of his flock, and of their fat. And the Lord had respect to Abel and to his offerings; but to Cain and his offerings he had no respect. And Cain was exceedingly angry, and his countenance fell." On the altar of Abel a lamb is being consumed, the smoke of which ascends between the extended arms of the innocent youth, and forms a cloud, on which reposes a figure of the Eternal Father, who, with hand extended towards the altar, seems "to have respect to Abel's offering." On the left is the figure of Cain, crouching rather than kneeling, his fallen countenance averted from his altar, on which are being consumed fruits of the earth. The smoke ascends ungracefully, and forms a cloud emerging from which is seen a horned figure of Lucifer. This window is "From Charles and John Johnston."

The subject of the next window is

THE SACRIFICE OF NOE.

The patriarch and family are represented as offering sacrifice to God in thanksgiving for their deliverance. The Scriptural account gives the key to the whole scene: "And Noe built an altar unto the Lord; and taking all cattle and fowls that were clean, offered holocausts upon the altar." In the midst of the prayerful group is an altar on which burns a lamb, and the foreground is strewn with sacrificial knife, vessels of blood, and slain beasts and fowl ready to be consumed. In the background oxen, asses, and deer are browsing on the hillside, while in the distance rises Mount Ararat, and on its summit rests the ark, around which flocks of birds are circling, and, enclosing all, the rainbow shines out conspicuously. The effect of the rainbow, as seen at night when the interior of the Cathedral is illuminated, is something remarkable.

This window is awaiting a donor.

The adjoining window represents

THE SACRIFICE OF MELCHISEDECH.

Here is beautifully portrayed the scene that took place in "the woodland vale which now is the salt sea," when "Melchisedech, the King of Salem, bringing forth bread and wine, for he was the priest of the most high God, blessed Abram, and said: Blessed be Abram by the most high God, who created heaven and earth." In the foreground is seen the majestic form of Melchisedech in regal attire, holding in his hands a smoking censer, and in the act of incensing the offering of bread and wine before him, in which was so literally foreshadowed the Sacrifice of the Mass. Around him stand Abram and a group of armed warriors, just returned from victory. In the tracery above this scene an angel keeps watch, and around the circle that incloses it is the legend in Latin, "Thou art a priest forever according to the order of Melchisedech."

This window is also awaiting a donor.

The first window on the south side of the sanctuary represents

THE SACRIFICE OF ABRAHAM.

The three figures, the angel, Abraham and Isaac, fill the foreground. On a rude altar of wood and pile of faggots the boy, with hands bound, reclines, his countenance not betraying the least suspicion of harm. A vessel filled with fire stands ready near the altar to consume the human sacrifice, while the patriarch "has taken the sword to sacrifice his son, and behold an angel of the Lord called to him, saying: Abraham! Abraham! lay not thy hand upon the boy." The face of the "father of the faithful" is full of astonishment, showing admirably the depth of his conviction that God must be obeyed, even though an angel should forbid. The calm expression of the angel forms a striking contrast with that of the patriarch, as the former stays the stroke gently with one hand, and with the other points to "a ram amongst the briars, sticking fast by the horns." In the background is a well wrought out mountain scene in "the land of vision."

This window is the "Gift of Daniel J. Murphy, San Francisco."

The subject of the next window is

THE EATING OF THE PASCHAL LAMB.

Here we have the interior of a Hebrew household. The time is the night of the institution of the feast of the Passover, in the land of Egypt. The father of the family with uplifted hands and eyes is engaged in profound prayer, in which the other members unite, as they stand around the board, their loins girt, shoes on their feet and holding staves in their hands, while a slave bears in the paschal, lamb, "roasted whole, with the head and feet and entrails thereof." A boy is seated at his father's feet, deeply intent on fastening his sandal for a journey he must soon make. At the door is seen a female sprinkling the door-cheeks with "a bunch of hyssop, steeped in the blood of the lamb, that he who destroyed the first-born might not touch them," whilst out against the dark night sky is seen the destroying angel speeding on his errand of destruction.

This window also awaits a donor's name.

The sixth and last of the windows of the Sacrifice represents that of which all the others were but types and figures—the great Sacrifice of Calvary. In the distance rises the Mount of Calvary, with three naked crosses standing out against the sky. The sacrifice is over, Christ has been laid in the tomb. The sun of justice is rising behind Calvary. An allegorical figure of Error is seen fleeing into the night, surrounded by owls and bats and the emblems of darkness, and stumbling over the *débris* of broken altars and implements of Pagan worship. In the foreground rises an allegorical figure of Truth, who, with uplifted cross, rules the world. Before this figure stands an altar on which a kneeling form is placing the noblest offering ever made to Truth in this hemisphere. The figure is that of his Eminence the Cardinal Archbishop of New York; the offering is the new St. Patrick's Cathedral. This window bears on it an inscription commemorating the date of his Eminence's creation as Cardinal, March 15, 1875

It is the "Gift of John Laden."

The idea of the above six windows of the Sacrifice guarding the grand altar on which the most adorable sacrifice of the Mass is to be offered will be recognized as one of the happiest conceptions in connection with the Cathedral. These windows will stand, we trust, for ages, as living witnesses to the fact that a priesthood, an altar, and a sacrifice have ever been essential elements in the worship of God.

We now come to the windows of the apse.

The subject of the first of these, beginning on the south side, in order to follow here also the chronological order, is

THE RESURRECTION OF LAZARUS.

The scene represented is that which took place when our Lord " cried with a loud voice : 'Lazarus ! come forth.'" With one hand Christ is pointing toward heaven, as if the echo of his prayer, " Father, I give Thee thanks that Thou hast heard me," still lingered in the air. With the other he points to Lazarus, and seems to order those present " to loose him and let him go." The face of Lazarus is the best meditation on death we have ever seen painted. He is verily a risen corpse " of now four days." He is kneeling at the entrance of the sepulchre, with the expression of one called suddenly from a deep sleep, half doubting, half dreaming. Behind him stands a male friend who is in the act of removing the napkin that is bound about his head. An aged female is wrapped in prayer, and at her side, kneeling at the feet of the Master, is Martha with a look of unutterable fear mingled with joy.

This window is the " Gift of Miss Ann Eliza McLaughlin."

THE COMMUNION OF ST. JOHN.

In this window is represented the scene at the Last Supper when Jesus took bread, and blessed and broke, and gave to his disciples and said : " Take ye and eat : *this is my body.*" " The disciple whom Jesus loved" is kneeling in the foreground, his eyes fixed on the Saviour's face, who, standing, is in the act of presenting His Sacred Body with His right hand to St. John, and in his left holding a chalice. Around the Supper-table, in the background, are five of the apostles looking on with wrapt attention. The window is a most appropriate offering and subject to commemorate the first communion of the donor, Miss Mamie Caldwell.

The central window of the apse presents the scene of

THE RESURRECTION OF OUR LORD.

This window justly occupies the most conspicuous site in the sanctuary, as its subject is the hinge on which all our faith turns. "If Christ be not risen then our preaching is vain, and your faith also is vain" It contains also the best executed figure of Our Blessed Lord in the whole collection of stained glass. Our Lord is rising from the tomb, and bears in his right hand a bright banner, on which a cross is emblazoned. The face and form are full of calm dignity and grace. Beneath the risen Saviour two of the guards are taking to flight, while a third has fallen down with fear, a picture of abject helplessness. An angel, bearing a palm branch, is tranquilly seated on the stone that has been rolled back from the mouth of the sepulchre, and is awaiting the coming of "Mary Magdalen, Joanna, and Mary the mother of James," who are seen approaching in the distance.

This window is inscribed, "From the Diocese of Buffalo."

The subject of the fourth window of the apse is

THE GIVING OF THE KEYS TO ST. PETER.

Our Lord is standing, and in the act of addressing to the Prince of the Apostles the words, " Thou art Peter, and I will give to thee the keys of the kingdom of heaven." With his right hand the Saviour presents the keys, and with his left points to heaven, as if to remind Peter of the account to be rendered there. The apostle, kneeling in an attitude of deep humility, hears the promise of the great trust to be committed to him—the government of the universal church.

Six other disciples are witnesses of the scene. In the distance a mountain landscape, and on the summit of one, are seen the towers and battlements of a city, an allusion to the words "the kingdom of God is like to a city seated on a mountain."

This window is the "Gift of the Diocese of Brooklyn."

The fifth and last window of the apse represents

JESUS MEETING THE DISCIPLES GOING TO EMMAUS.

The risen Saviour is reproaching the disciples' incredulity with the words: "O foolish and slow of heart to believe. Ought not Christ to have suffered these things, and so to have entered into his glory?" It is the beginning of the journey, as appears from the fact that they have just come out of Jerusalem, whose gate, walls, and battlements, are seen near by. In the distance, turning an angle of the high-road, is seen a horseman, with servant on foot, reminding one of the good Samaritan. The expression of our Lord's face is full of sweetness, while that of the disciples is full of tender remorse for having, for a moment, wavered in their faith.

This window is inscribed: *"In memoriam W. M."*

Space would not permit us to enter into the description of the tracery of these windows, which teem with beautifully executed figures of angels, and texts from Scripture.

If it be asked why spend so much on details that can not be seen, we reply in the words of Pugin, who was lavish of pains on the least detail of his work, "God sees it."

Before quitting the sanctuary we will bend our steps toward the Lady Chapel. The window in the first bay represents the Presentation of the Blessed Virgin in the Temple. The high-priest, in gorgeous vesture, advances to receive the child, while St. Joachim

and St. Anne modestly remain standing behind. The friends of
the family are assembled to witness the ceremony. This bears the
inscription, "John Kelly, in memoriam."

The Adoration of the Child Jesus.—The Shepherds crowd around,
some on bended knee; on the opposite side the Magi approach,
bearing their precious gifts. This is the "Gift of Thomas H.
O'Connor."

Finally, the Blessed Virgin exposes to our veneration the Infant
after His birth. The face of the Mother is admirable. This window is the "Gift of Mrs. Julia Coleman."

THE WINDOWS OF THE TRANSEPT.

Having described the windows of the Sanctuary, we turn now to
the southern arm of the transept, where we meet, first:

THE WINDOW OF ST. LOUIS, KING OF FRANCE.

Here we have presented to us a memorable event in the life of
that Saint. He had rendered great services to Baldwin, Emperor
of Constantinople, and received from him in return the gift of many
precious relics of our Lord's Passion. To receive these sacred relics
worthily, the King built the Sainte Chapelle of Paris. The subject, then, is the solemn procession in which the relics are borne to
their resting place. In the foreground is seen the Saint, bearing
on a richly embroidered cushion the Crown of Thorns; on either
side walk two prelates, bearing each a jeweled casket containing,
one of them a portion of the True Cross, the other the Nails. All
three walk barefoot, and over them is borne a rich canopy of royal
purple, shot with the golden *fleur de lis* of France. Behind the
King is seen Queen Blanche, his mother, surrounded by nobles
wearing the coronets distinctive of their rank. The artist has

succeeded admirably in imparting to every face an expression of devotional reverence.

Underneath is the inscription, " From Henry L. Hoguet. "

Adjoining this is

THE WINDOW OF THE SACRED HEART.

In this scene our Lord is represented standing on the predella of an altar. Clouds encircle his feet, and cherubs hover around Him. Before Him Blessed Margaret Mary is kneeling, looking in ecstasy at the heart of Jesus, to which He points, an expression of ineffable tenderness lighting up His face. An angel stands in the background, holding a scroll, on which we read the words: *"Voilà le cœur que tant aime les hommes"*—Behold the heart that loves men so much. Behind Blessed Margaret is a nun, kneeling at a priedieu, reading attentively. The whole is a happy rendering of the apparition which has given such an impetus to the beautiful devotion of the Sacred Heart.

The window is " From Mrs. Eleanora Iselin. "

Passing next to the north transept, we find on the same line, first:

ST. PAUL'S WINDOW.

The Apostle of the Gentiles is here represented preaching before the sages of the Areopagus. His action is full of the well-known energy of St. Paul's character. With arms outstretched between heaven and his hearers, he has startled the novelty-loving Athenians into listening, by his bold exordium, " Ye men of Athens, I perceive that in all things ye are too superstitious. For passing by and seeing your idols, I found an altar also on which was written : *To the unknown God.* What, therefore, you worship without knowing it, that I preach to you. " On the faces of the venerable group before him are written all stages of belief, from doubt to deepest conviction, as they stand or sit in every attitude of profound attention. Prominent amongst them is seen one on whose noble features is stamped an expression of faith and goodness which marks him as no other than Dionysius the Areopagite, the most distinguished of the Athenian converts, who, the same tradition says, afterward preached the faith in Gaul and founded the church of Paris.

Viewed from an artistic standpoint, the heads of the Grecian elders are studies worthy of a master, and the whole scene is instinct with life.

This window bears the inscription: "To the memory of Rev. John Kelly, from his brother Eugene."

Adjoining this is

THE WINDOW OF ST. AUGUSTINE AND ST. MONICA.

St. Augustine stands by the deathbed of his mother, St. Monica. His head is bowed down in sadness as he listens to the last wishes of her who has been to him twice a mother. Her last injunction is, "My son, when I am dead lay this body anywhere, but remember me always at the altar of God." An attendant is raising the arm of the dying Saint, with which she seems about to bless, for the last time, her son. Around the apartment stand weeping friends and attendants. In the distance is seen a view of Ostia-on-the-Tiber where the Saint died.

This window bears the inscription: "From Mamie and Lina Caldwell in memory of their parents."

ST. MATHEW'S WINDOW.

It is located on the east side of the north transept door. A life-size figure of the Evangelist, with pen in one hand and book of his Gospel in the other, occupies the central bay. Beneath him is the distinctive symbol of St. Mathew, the figure of an angel. The two lateral bays are filled with four scenes from the life of the Saint. These are: 1. St. Mathew's Vocation, in which our Lord is represented saying to him, "Follow me;" 2. He preaches the Gospel in Ethiopia; 3. He raises the King's Son from the dead; 4. The Saint's Martyrdom.

This window is the "Gift of Andrew Clarke."

On the west side of the same door we find

ST. MARK'S WINDOW.

The figure of the Evangelist, with pen and book, the winged lion of St. Mark reposing at his feet, fills the central bay of this window. Four scenes from the Saint's life fill the two side bays. These are: 1. Writing the Gospel in company with St. Peter; 2. He builds the Church of St. Peter, Alexandria; 3. Our Lord appears to him in Prison; 4. His Martyrdom.

This window is the "Gift of Bernard Maguire.

In the south transept, on the west side of the entrance, is

ST. LUKE'S WINDOW.

Here, too, the central bay is occupied by the figure of the Evangelist, with the customary pen and book, and beneath is the figure of an ox, the emblem of St. Mark. The four scenes from the life of the Saint that fill the two remaining bays are: 1. He is writing his Gospel in company with St. Paul; 2. His preaching and conversions in the Thebaid; 3. He paints the portrait of the Blessed Virgin; 4. His Martyrdom.

This window is the "Gift of Denis J. Dwyer."

ST. JOHN'S WINDOW

occupies the corresponding position on the east side of the south transept door. The Evangelist, holding as usual the pen and book, an eagle, the emblem of St. John, perched at his feet, is the central figure of this window. The four scenes from the Saint's life, are: 1. He is reposing on the bosom of Our Lord; 2. He, in company with St. Peter, cures the Cripple at the "Beautiful Gate" of the Temple, saying: "In the Name of Jesus, arise and walk:" 3. He converts the Young Man who had become an Outlaw; 4. He is writing his Apocalypse.

This window is the "Gift of William Joyce."

The above-named four windows are the work of Mr. Ely of Nantes.

On the west wall of the north transept is

THE WINDOW OF ST. CHARLES BORROMEO.

The saintly cardinal, bearing a crucifix, advances in solemn procession from the door of the Cathedral of Milan. Before him lie prostrate two victims of the plague. One of the figures is that of a mother, to whom clings a distracted child. It is a most graphic description of the horrors of the plague. Below is represented the scene of the dissolute monk firing at the cardinal while conducting evening prayer in his private chapel. This window is the "Gift of Lorenzo Delmonico."

On the west wall of the south transept is

THE WINDOW OF ST. PATRICK,

designed and presented by the architect. It is of particular interest, on account of the subjects introduced. St. Patrick is represented preaching to an assembly of peasants, whose faces are admirable types of Celtic character. In the distance is seen a primitive wooden church in process of erection. The scene underneath represents the architect submitting his plan to Archbishop Hughes, who is seated at a table. His Eminence Cardinal McCloskey stands in the foreground, holding the diagram of that part of the building which he has altered from the original plan. Behind His Eminence stands M. Lorin, the maker of the window, and a few religious who furnished the historical scenes that have been so vividly realized in the various windows throughout the Cathedral. The portraits are excellent, and so perfect are the details that on a portfolio resting against the table may be read : " James Renwick, Esq., New York. "

Turning now towards the " long drawn aisles " there remain ten windows which merit a more detailed description than the space allotted to us will permit. However, owing to their proximity to the spectator, their many, even the least, beauties are within easy view. Beginning on the north, or gospel side, at the angle of the transept, we meet first with

ST. BERNARD'S WINDOW.

The scene here laid before us is St. Bernard preaching the Second Crusade. Habited in the simple white robe of the Cistercian Order, with shaven crown, the cross uplifted in one hand, the other resting on his breast and his eyes raised to heaven, the figure of St. Bernard forms a striking contrast to the group around him. Mail-clad warriors of every age, from maturity upward, listen eagerly to the burning words of the greatest preacher of his time. The effect of the Saint's thrilling eloquence on his hearers is seen in the eager gestures of the leaders amongst them, many of whom are offering their drawn swords to heaven, as if pleading to be allowed to fight the battle of God. The picture is full of life, and the treatment of this subject is historically correct.

This window is the " Gift of the Diocese of Rochester."

The subject of the next window is

THE MARTYRDOM OF ST. LAWRENCE.

The figure of the martyr, on which all the interest of this scene centres, is considered by all who have seen it a masterpiece. The

Saint is stretched on a gridiron ; a glowing fire blazes beneath him ; his *Acts* tell us that " his face appeared to be surrounded with an extraordinary light, and his broiled body to exhale a sweet, agreeable smell." His eyes are turned toward the cruel judge who directs the barbarous execution, and to whom he seems to say, with a smiling countenance, as his *Acts* relate : " Let my body be now turned; one side is broiled enough." The savage cruelty of the judge's expression is in marked contrast to the meekness of the martyr's look. The crouching figure of the executioner in the foreground, as he plies his horrid work, is a study.

This window is the "Gift of the Diocese of Ogdensburgh." Adjoining this is

THE WINDOW OF THE BROTHERS OF THE CHRISTIAN SCHOOLS.

The scene represented here is the Papal approbation of the Constitution of the Brothers of the Christian Schools, by Benedict XIII., January 26th, 1725.

The Pope is seated on a throne, and in the act of receiving from Brother Timothy, Superior General, a volume, supported on a richly embroidered cushion, and containing the Rules of the Society. The faces of the assembled Brothers are full of intense anxiety, as the event is for them full of the deepest interest. Their dark habits contrast strikingly with the bright uniforms of the members of the Papal court.

The window is the "Gift of the Christian Brothers."

The next is one of the brightest pictures in the Cathedral: it is

THE WINDOW OF ST. COLUMBANUS.

The subject of this painting is briefly this, as related in Cantu's " Universal History : " Thierry II, King of Burgundy, led a life that was the scandal of his kingdom. He had often, but to no purpose, been rebuked and threatened by his own clergy. St. Columbanus, though a comparative stranger, had but a few years before migrated from Ireland and founded a monastery near the palace of the King. The latter, hearing of the Saint's austerities, and wishing to be on friendly terms with him, visited the monastery, bringing with him rich presents of delicate viands and wine. In the scene presented to us the Saint meets the King at the door of the monastery, rebukes him for his scandalous life, and with a blow strikes from the hand of the attendant the rare vessel of wine, saying: " God rejects the gifts of the wicked, nor ought they to pollute the lips of the servant of God." The King is at once converted, becomes contrite, and humbly sues to be reconciled to the Church. Behind the King is seen the stately figure of Brunichilda, whose nuptials had never been blessed by the Church, but who had been to Thierry as Queen. She, having prayed the Saint to bless her offspring, receives for answer, " No ; and of them none shall ever wield the sceptre of his father, because they are the children of sin." The proud woman is seen retreating, with a gesture of reprobation, toward her converted husband, regarding the monk with a look of intense hatred. The scene would require pages to do it justice.

This window is inscribed : " In memory of Daniel Devlin, from his brothers Jeremiah and William."

The four above-named windows are the work of M. Lorin.

The last in this, the north aisle, is

THE WINDOW OF THE THREE BAPTISMS.

The three baptisms are, as termed in theology, the baptism of water, the baptism of blood—by martyrdom, and the baptism of desire—when no one is near to administer the sacrament, and the soul ardently desires it. These are three gates through some one of which all must enter into the City of God who are to be saved. This window is appropriately placed near the main entrance, and over the chapel of the baptistery. In the central bay is the scene of our Lord's baptism by St. John, the baptism of water; to the right is the scene of a martyrdom, and in the left bay a solitary reclining figure dying with a desire to be baptized, to " be dissolved and be with Christ.

This window is the " Gift of James McKenna."

Crossing now to the south aisle we first meet with

ST. VINCENT DE PAUL'S WINDOW.

In the central division of this window stands a life-size figure of the Saint, habited in stole and surplice. The expression on his benign countenance is all we would look for on the face of the messenger of charity. The two scenes in the lateral bays give the two grand features of his life—his devotion to homeless children and to the worst class of criminals. On the right hand the Saint is represented calmly seated whilst the ball-and-chain of a galley-slave is made fast to his foot. The prisoner whose punishment the holy man has taken on him is seen going on his way rejoicing. On the left St. Vincent is holding an infant in his arms, while he directs the attention of a Sister of Charity to another little waif asleep on the pavement.

This window is the " Gift of James Olwell."

The two last-mentioned windows are from the studio of M. Ely of Nantes. We next come to

THE WINDOW OF ST. ELIZABETH, ST. ANDREW, AND ST. CATHERINE.

The three bays of this window are filled, each with an admirably executed life-size figure of one of these saints. St. Andrew the Apostle holds the place of honor in the centre. He is represented as if in the act of taking upon him the cross on which he, like St. Peter, had the glory of receiving the martyr's crown. The expression on his furrowed features is one of calm courage, which seems to come to him from heaven, on which his uplifted eyes are fixed. Beneath him is a finished miniature, if we may be allowed to so name anything so large, representing the scene of the martyr's execution. The same face is recognizable in this as that of the larger figure above, notwithstanding the difference of dimensions. In the right compartment of the window is the figure of St. Catherine, of Alexandria, martyr. She holds in one hand the palm branch of victory, and with the other leans on a wheel, the instrument of her cruel torture and glorious death. Beneath is a beautiful and graphic rendering of the espousals of St. Catherine to our Lord, which Rubens has made so memorable. The Infant Jesus is seated on the lap of his Virgin mother, and, smiling sweetly, places a ring on the finger of the Saint, who is kneeling at the feet of the Virgin. This reward the Saint received in a vision, after having vowed her virginity to Christ. In the left bay is a figure of equal size with the others—of St. Elizabeth, Queen of Hungary. Her eyes are cast down, looking in wonder at the miracle God has performed in her behalf. The object of her regard is a bouquet of exquisite flowers, which she holds in the folds of her mantle. Beneath the figure is the explanation. St. Elizabeth, who loves the good poor exceedingly, is here represented, after the true history, as told in her life by Montalembert, as carrying bread to some of her clients, when she is met by her husband, who has had unjust suspicions. He insists on seeing what his spouse carries so carefully concealed; she unfolds her mantle, when lo! the bread has turned to flowers. This was heaven's approbation of the Saint's charity and rebuke to her husband.

This window is inscribed, "From the family of J. A. and Eliza O'Reilly."

The adjoining window is regarded by all as one of the chastest designs in the Cathedral; its subject is

THE ANNUNCIATION.

The Blessed Virgin is here represented kneeling: her countenance does not betray a shadow of surprise at the appearance of her angelic visitor, who, with a look of profound respect, is in the act of delivering the message which has brought so much "Glory to God on high and peace on earth to men." The interior of the house of Nazareth is evidently copied in all its details from the Holy House of Loretto, as any one who has seen the latter will at once recognize. Through the door, which is partially concealed by a half-drawn curtain, is seen St. Joseph in his carpenter shop, discussing, doubtless, the details of some little household improvement, pertaining to his trade, with an elderly female. The same peace and silence appear to reign over the simple scene without, as over the momentous one taking place within between God's messenger and God's mother soon to be. The position this window occupies throws it out in greater relief, and lends it new attractions, as the visitor will at once realize when, passing from the turbulent field of battle, his eye rests on the peaceful home of Nazareth.

This window is the "Gift of William and John O'Brien."

We next come to

ST. HENRY'S WINDOW.

This is a battle-piece that, it has been said, would do honor to the Louvre. The subject of the window is the battle fought by St. Henry, Emperor of Germany, against the Sclavonians, who had risen up against the ecclesiastical authorities, put to death priests, and drove bishops from their Sees, and generally laid waste the fair land of Poland. The aid of the Emperor was invoked, who,

ever willing to raise his arm in the cause of God, went to the assist-
ance of the distressed. The enemy outnumbered the Emperor's
troops by thousands. The Saint, however, did not lose heart. He
heard Mass early in the morning, at which all his troops devoutly
assisted, and, invoking the blessing of the God of battles on his
arms, went forth fearlessly to victory. That no assurance of tri-
umph might be wanting to him, God vouchsafed to reveal to him the
presence, in the field, of St. Lawrence, St. Adrian, and St. George,
fighting on the side of the Emperor. This painting needs no com-
ment. It is instinct with life and "movement," as artists say.

This window is the "Gift of Henry J. Anderson."

The last window that remains for us to speak of is

THE WINDOW OF THE IMMACULATE CONCEPTION.

The scene which this window portrays is the memorable one which
took place in Rome in the year 1854, when the late beloved Pontiff, Pius IX., proclaimed to the world the dogma of the Immaculate
Conception. The Sovereign Pontiff is standing on his throne after
having proclaimed the dogma, *urbi et orbi,* and in the act of giving
the apostolic benediction, while he holds in his left hand the decree
of the dogma. The well-known, benign features of the lamented
Pius are easily recognized. The surrounding group is a good
representation of the Church. Here we have cardinals, patriarchs,
bishops, prelates, priests and religious of several orders in the
distinctive habits of their congregations. The bright costumes of
the Papal household troops give additional animation to the scene.
Above the head of the Pope is a figure of the Immaculate Conception. The statues of Sts. Peter and Paul, on either side will
be recognized by all who have seen the originals as admirable
reproductions of the two magnificent statues of the apostles, that
stand guardians of the entrance to St. Peter's, Rome.

This window is the "Gift of the Diocese of Newark."

The beautiful oil paintings in the north and south transepts, representing "The Baptism of Our Lord," "The Marriage Feast of Cana," "The Return of the Prodigal Son," and "St. Patrick preaching at Tara," were presented by Hon. John Kelly, New York.

——————✠——————

THE ORGANS.

The grand organ is placed in a gallery in the first bay of the nave, between the front towers. This gallery is capable of accommodating a choir of one hundred singers. It is 46 feet in width, across the building, and 2S feet long; and is supported in front by a wrought iron compound girder, 3 feet 9 inches in depth, 14 inches in width, and capable of sustaining a weight of 100 tons. The front of the organ gallery is of ash, supported by moulded and carved brackets of the same material, projecting from and attached to the great iron beam. The ceiling of the gallery is divided into squares by rich mouldings of ash, and the squares are filled with 2 inch strips of ash, laid on diagonally. Access to it is had by means of a spiral staircase situated in the south lobby of the Fifth Avenue entrance. The organ was built under the direction of Rev. Father McMahon, rector of the church of St. John the Evangelist, in which church it has been used for some years past. The organ is one of the open style, displaying all the pipes, symmetrically grouped and highly decorated. It has four manuals and a compass of two and a half octaves in the pedals. It is an instrument of great power and variety of tone.

NOTE.—The account of the Cathedral is an abridgment of that furnished by Jas. Renwick, Esq., the architect. The compiler, in making a general acknowledgment to those from whom he has obtained his information, feels bound to record his special thanks to Wm. Joyce, Esq., the superintendent and builder, and to Mr. D. J. Dwyer, the assistant superintendent, for the very great kindness shown him. It is through these gentlemen that he has been able to give the public correct information regarding the various interior measurements, the altars, etc., etc., as they actually stand. For description of windows he is indebted to the full and beautiful contributions of Rev. J. M. Farley to the *Cathedral Fair Journal*. For biographical sketches the compiler is indebted to Rev. Alfred Young, C. S. P.

The Archbishops and Bishops

Present at the Ceremony of Dedication.

---✠---

Archbishops.

Most Rev. JAMES GIBBONS, D.D., Baltimore.
"   JOHN B. PURCELL, D.D., Cincinnati.
"   JAMES F. WOOD, D.D., Philadelphia.
"   JOHN J. WILLIAMS, D.D., Boston.
"   JOHN J. LYNCH, D.D., Toronto, Canada.
"   MICHAEL HANNAN, D.D., Halifax, Nova Scotia.

Bishops.

Province of New York.

Right Rev. John Loughlin, D.D., Brooklyn.
"   Bernard J. McQuaid, D.D., Rochester.
"   Stephen Vincent Ryan, C.M., D.D., Buffalo.
"   Francis McNeirny, D.D., Albany.
"   Edgar P. Wadhams, D.D., Ogdensburgh.
"   Michael A. Corrigan, D.D., Newark.
"   John J. Conroy, D.D., Curium.

Province of Baltimore.

Right Rev. P N. Lynch, D.D., Charleston.
"   Thomas A. Becker, D.D., Wilmington.
"   William H. Gross, D.D., Savannah.
"   J. J. Kain, D.D., Wheeling.
"   John Moore, D.D., St. Augustine.
"   John J. Keane, D.D., Richmond.

Province of New Orleans.

Right. Rev. John Quinlan, D.D., Mobile.

Province of Boston.

Right Rev. Louis de Goesbriand, D.D., Burlington.
" 	P. T. O'Reilly, D.D., Springfield.
" 	Thomas F. Hendricken, D.D., Providence.
" 	James A. Healey, D.D., Portland.

Province of Philadelphia.

Right Rev. Jeremiah F. Shanahan, D.D., Harrisburg.
" 	William O'Hara, D.D., Scranton.
" 	John Tuigg, D.D., Pittsburgh and Allegheny.

Province of St. Louis.

Right Rev. Patrick J. Ryan, D.D., St. Louis.
" 	James O'Connor, D.D., Vic. Ap., Nebraska.
" 	John L. Spalding, D.D., Peoria.

Province of Cincinnati.

Right Rev. Francis S. Chatard, D.D., Vincennes.

Province of Milwaukee.

Right Rev. John Ireland, D.D., Coadjutor-Bishop, St. Paul.

Province of Quebec.

Right Rev. Jos. Thomas Duhamel, D.D., Ottawa.

Province of Halifax.

Right Rev. John Sweeny, D.D., St. John, N. B.
" 	James Rogers, D.D., Chatham, N. B.

———

Right Rev. Mgr. Seton, D.D., Prothonotary-Apostolic.

The Celebrants

AND

THEIR MINISTERS, CANTORS, ETC.,

AT THE

Blessing, Solemn Mass, and Vespers.

--- ✠ ---

AT THE BLESSING AND MASS:

Celebrant: HIS EMINENCE JOHN CARDINAL MCCLOSKEY, Arch
bishop of New York.
Assistant Priest: V. Rev. William Quinn, V.G.
First Assist. Deacon: V. Rev. Thos. S. Preston, V.G.
Second Assist. Deacon: Rev. A. J. Donnelly.
Deacon of the Mass: Rev. Edward McGlynn, D.D.
Subdeacon of the Mass: Rev. Jas. H. McGean.

Masters of Ceremonies:

Rev. John F. Kearney.   Rev. H. C. Macdowall.
"   Felix H. Farrelly.   "   William Hogan.

Cantors for the Miserere :

Rev. John J. Kean.
" J. Dougherty.
" P. S. Rigney.
" W. A. Farrell.

Rev. John Reardon.
" Anthony Lammel.
" James Barry.
" Chas. O'Keeffe.

Cantors for the Litany :

Rev. John Morris.
" John M. Grady.
" Charles Colton.
" Anthony Lammel.
" Charles O'Keeffe.

Rev. James Barry.
" J. Dougherty.
" P. S. Rigney.
" John Reardon.
" John J. Kean.

Cantors for the Procession in the Cathedral :

Rev. John Reardon.
" John J. Kean.

Rev. J. Dougherty.
" Anthony Lammel.

THE SERMON AT MASS WAS PREACHED BY THE
RIGHT REV. PATRICK JOHN RYAN, D. D.,
Coadjutor-Bishop of the Archdiocese of St. Louis.

——✠——

AT VESPERS :

Celebrant : The Most Rev. JAMES GIBBONS, Archbishop of Baltimore.
Deacons : Rev. John J. Kean and Rev. Wm. Farrell.

Cope-Bearers :

Rev. Charles O'Keeffe.
" James Barry.
" John Reardon.

Rev. John Morris.
" P. S. Rigney.
" John M. Grady.

Masters of Ceremonies :

Rev. John F. Kearney.
" Charles C. McDonnell, D.D.

Cantors :

Rev. John McEvoy.
" James Barry.
" Charles O'Keeffe.
" P. S. Rigney.
" John Morris.
" John J. Kean.

Rev. John Reardon.
" John M. Grady.
" Charles Colton.
" W. A. Farrell.
" Anthony Lammel.
" J. Dougherty.

THE SERMON AT VESPERS WAS PREACHED BY THE
RIGHT REV. JOHN J. KEANE, D. D.
Bishop of Richmond.

www.ingramcontent.com/pod-product-compliance
Lightning Source LLC
Chambersburg PA
CBHW030719110426
42739CB00030B/920